All the places I've been...I feel like going home.

Home

jodi hills

Happy Birthday Sister ♡
2022

TRISTAN PUBLISHING
Minncapolis

To my mom's family.
You opened my heart to the rumor of home.
~jodi hills

Library of Congress Cataloging-in-Publication Data
Hills, Jodi, 1968-
Home / written by Jodi Hills.
    p. cm.
 ISBN 978-0-931674-50-1 (alk. paper)
 1. Home--Quotations, maxims, etc. I. Title.
 PN6084.H57H55 2012
 392.3--dc23
            2012006367

TRISTAN Publishing, Inc.
2355 Louisiana Avenue North
Golden Valley, MN 55427

All original paintings, acrylic on canvas.

Copyright © 2012, Jodi Hills
ISBN 978-0-931674-50-1
First Printing
Printed in China

To learn about all of our books with a message please visit
www.TRISTANpublishing.com

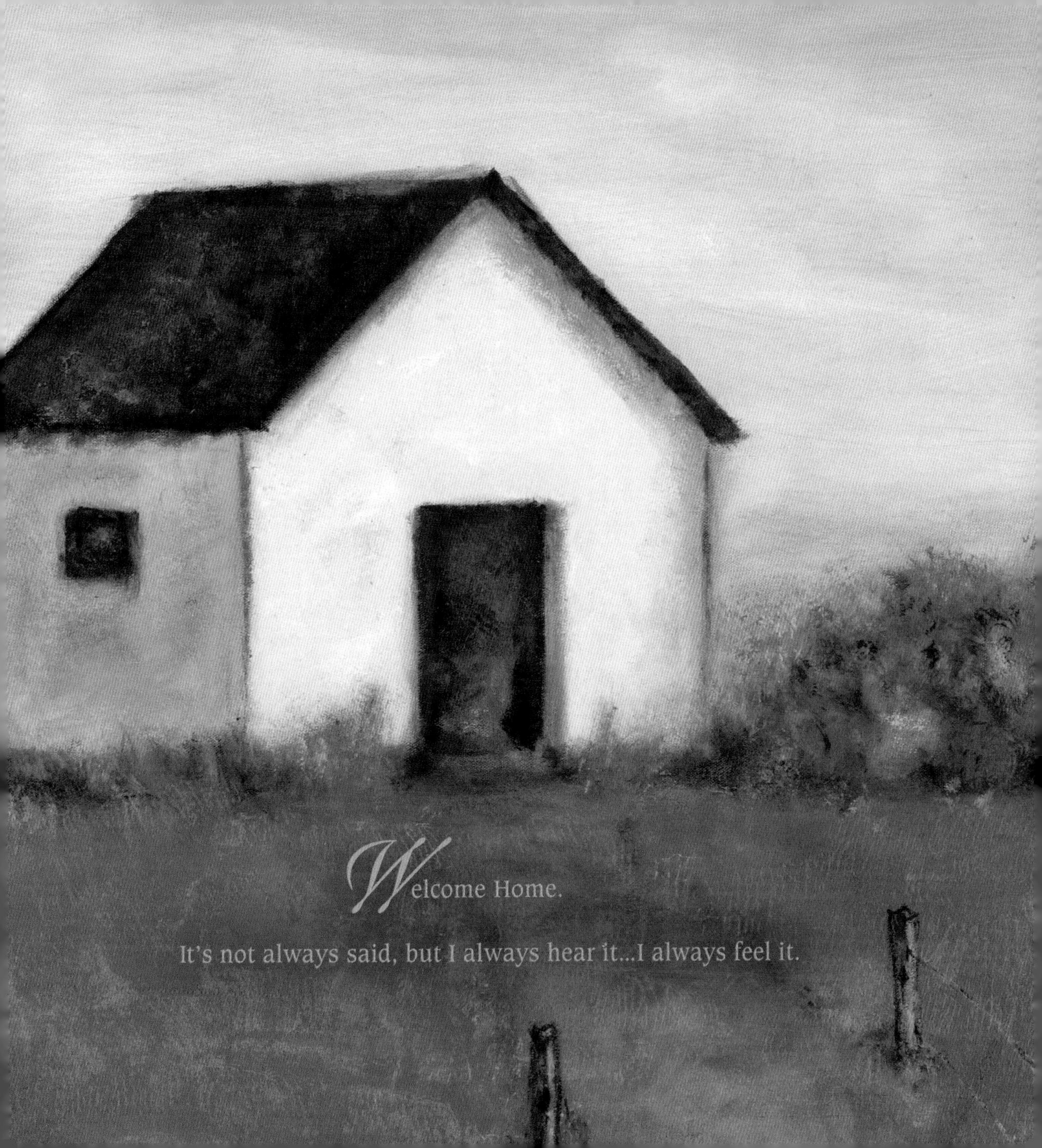

Welcome Home.

It's not always said, but I always hear it...I always feel it.

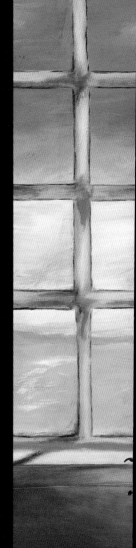

*H*ere, in the grasp of the doorknob,

the creak of the third step...

here, brushing against the coats hanging in line,

I feel it, and know that I am home.

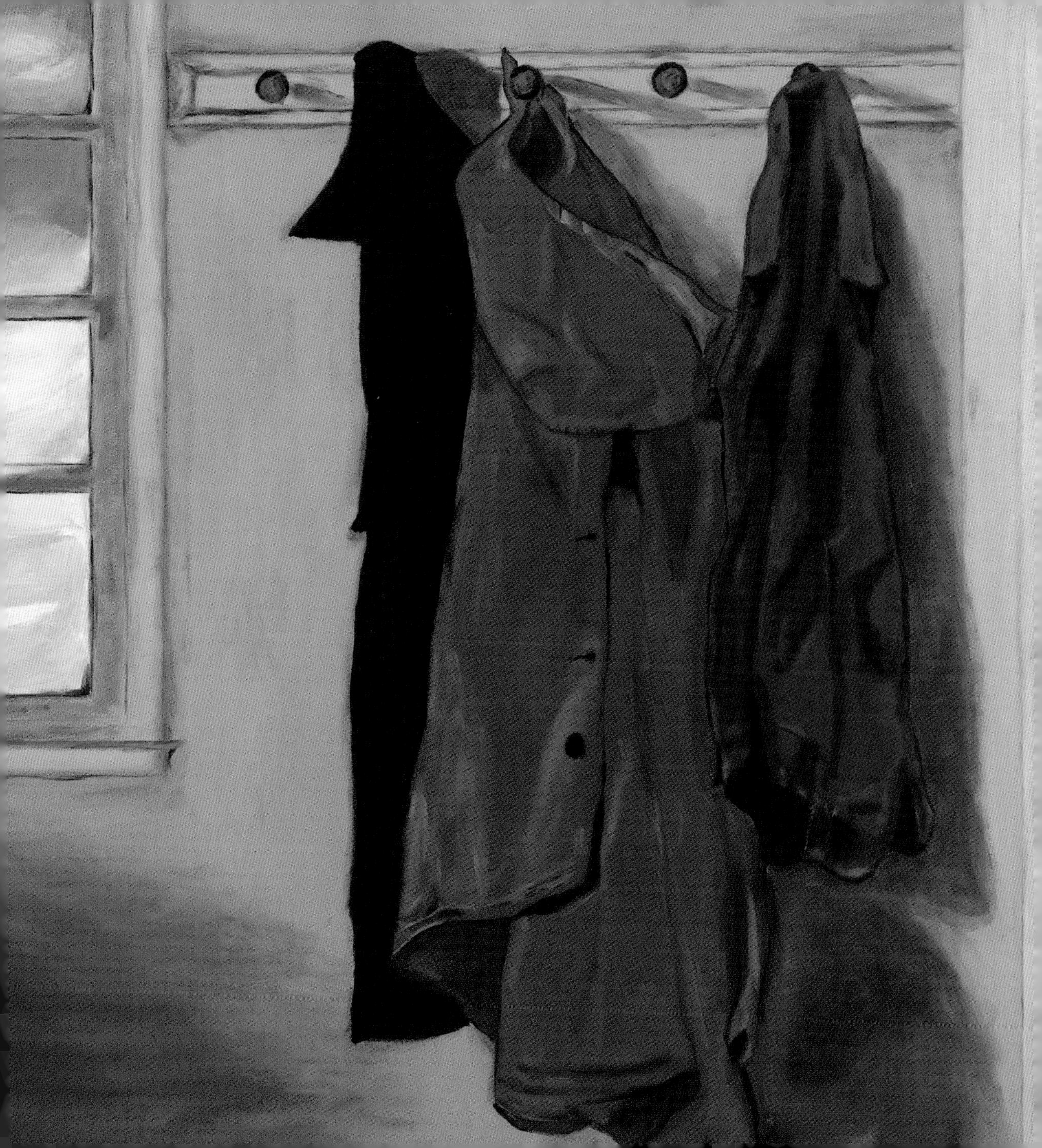

No emotion is ever turned away.

I can be happy or sad, or excited or tired...so I come.

Once the door is open, whatever I am, I am grateful.

I am happy to be home.

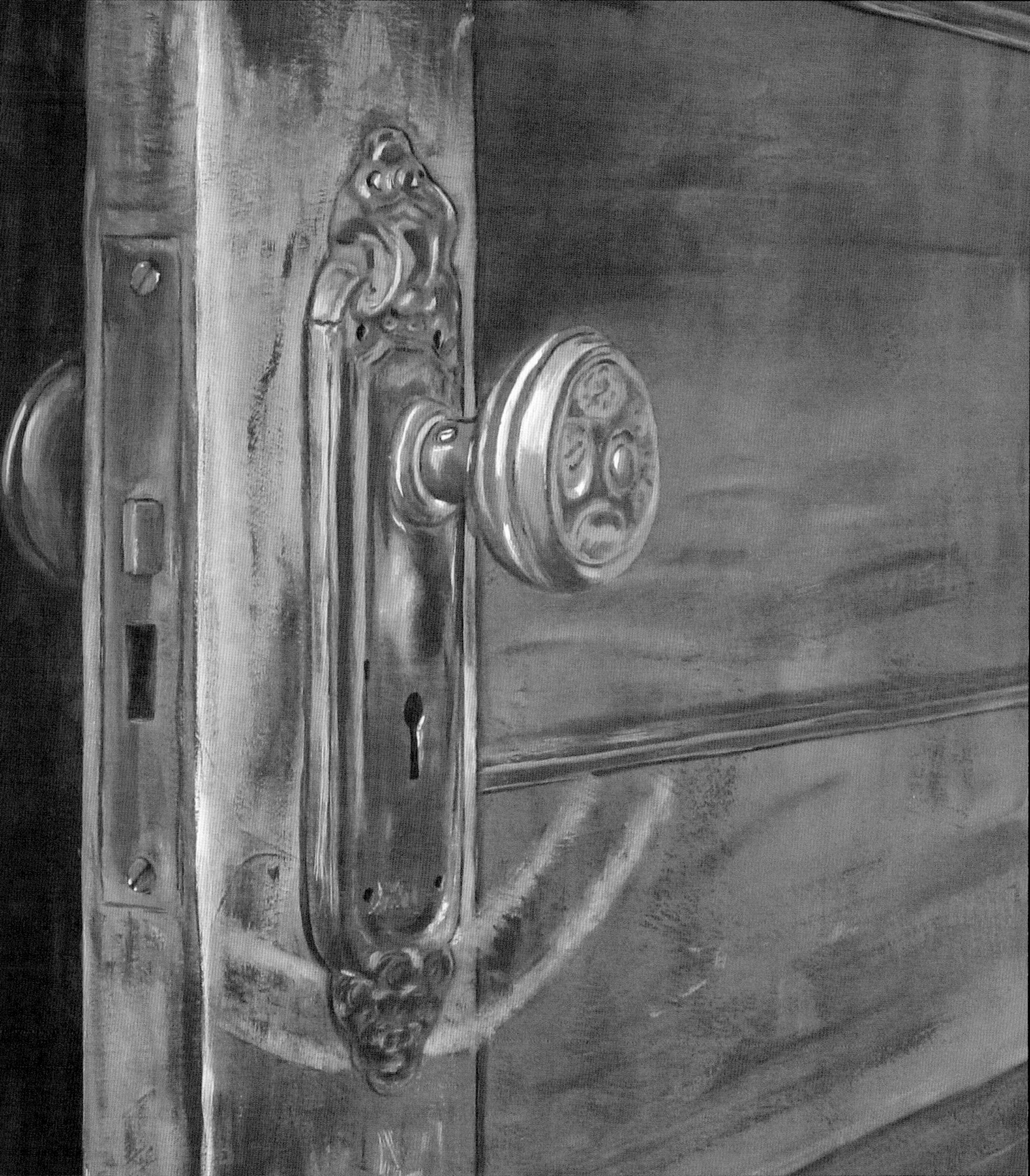

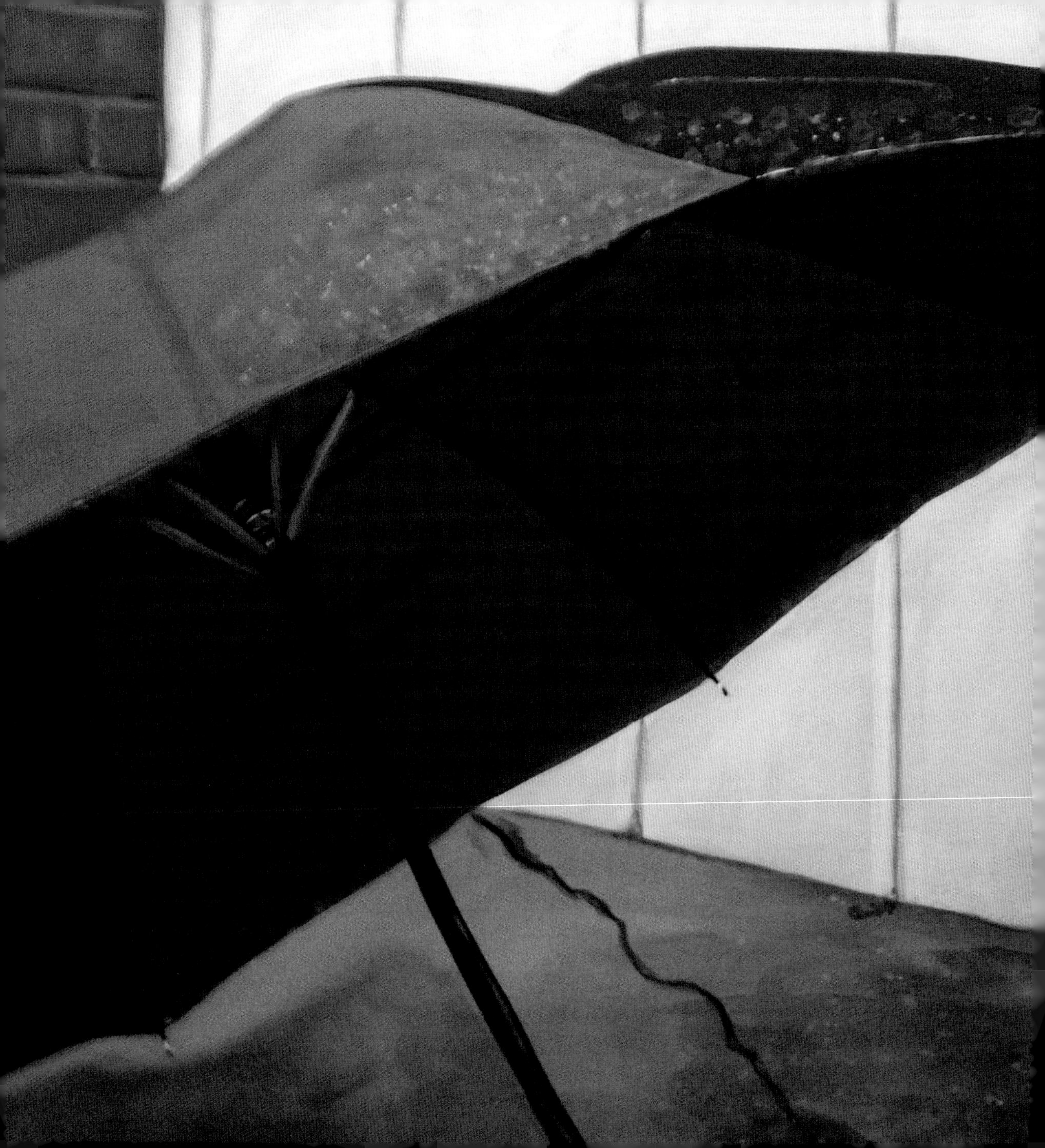

$\mathcal{I}$ come to this place in sunshine and rain.

Full and empty handed, I come.

The invitation is as open as its heart...and I come.

I come to this place that has seen me in every possible

flattering and unflattering light.

And it's not that I blend, but I belong.

Even alone, these walls hold a conversation. They speak of what I've seen, and what I've held. They echo parties and surprises, laughter and music...a conversation of lives.

These walls, like a best friend, allow me to join that conversation, or sit quietly in the warmth of memory and hopefully in the glow of possibility.

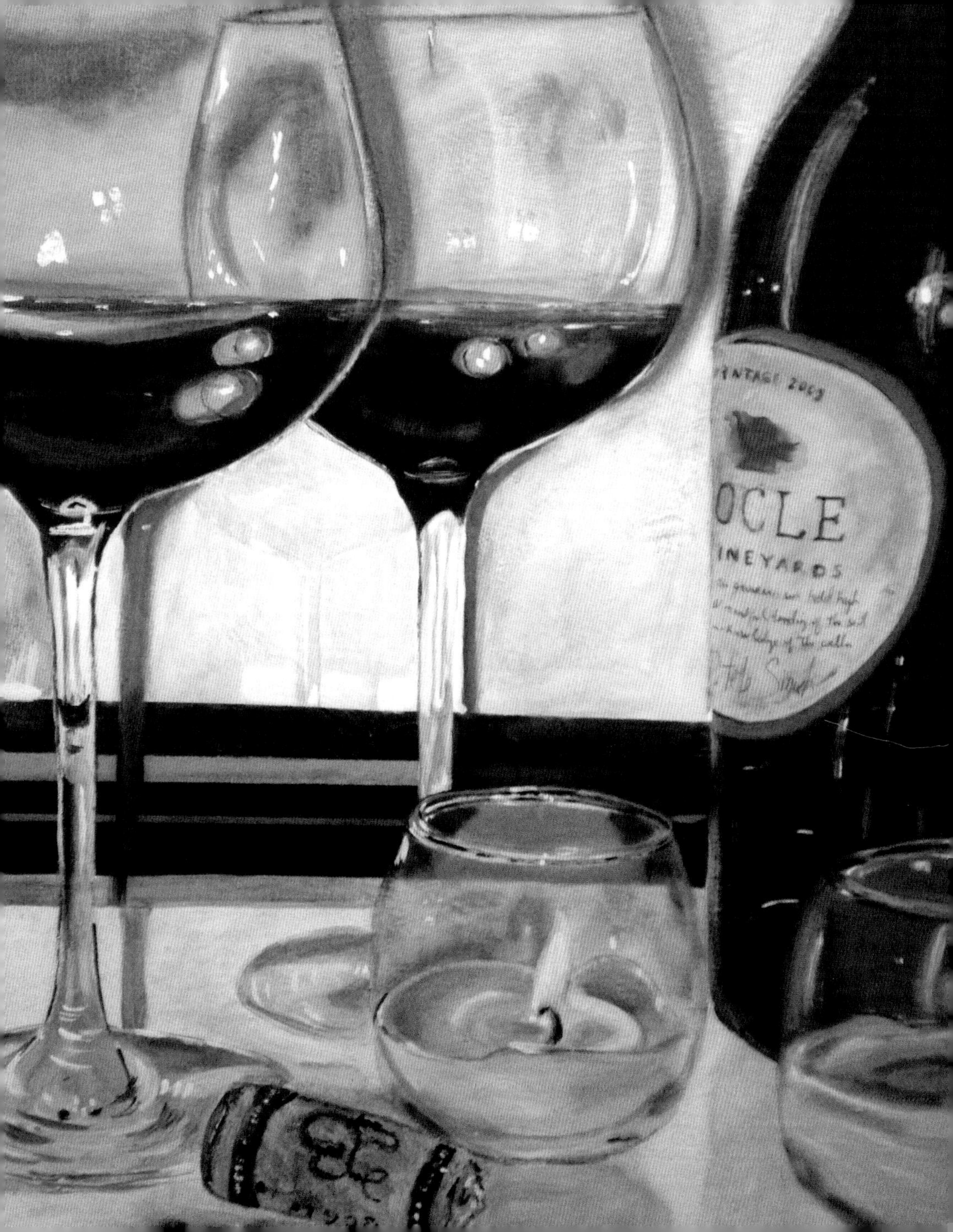
OCLE
INEYARDS

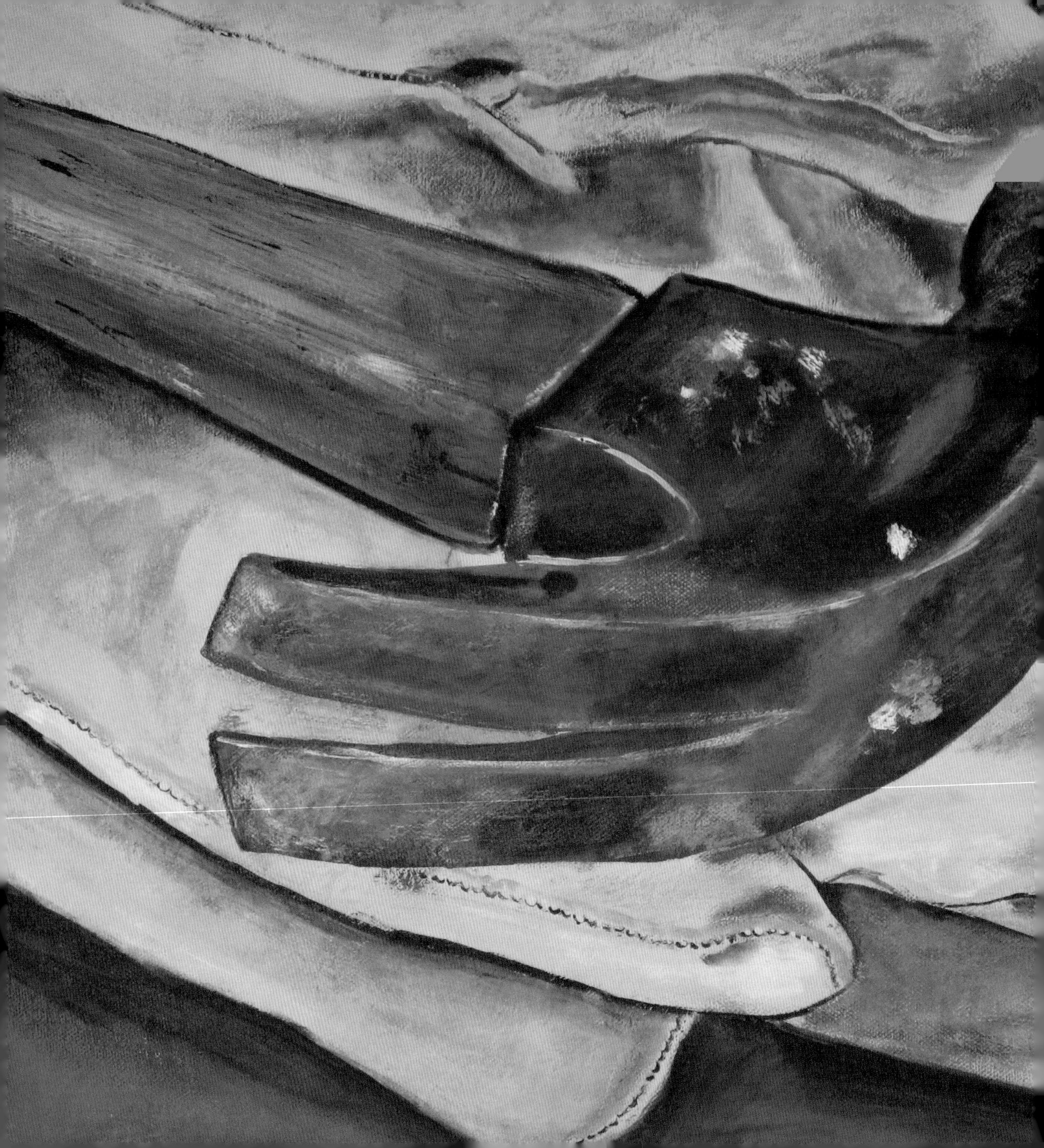

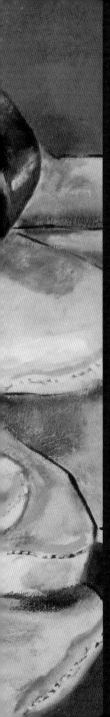

I come to this place that is stronger than pains of growth and winds of change, and the hammering of "unhandy" hands. Outliving impassioned, late night inspired renovations and holiday decorations. Withstanding beginnings and endings...it is built strong, and I come.

$\mathcal{I}$n a world of change, the smell of familiar leads me,

and I come. A truth beckons me. Unopened mail lures me.

A friendly palette gathers me. A warm light nestles me.

This simmering mix of relaxation and expectation envelops me.

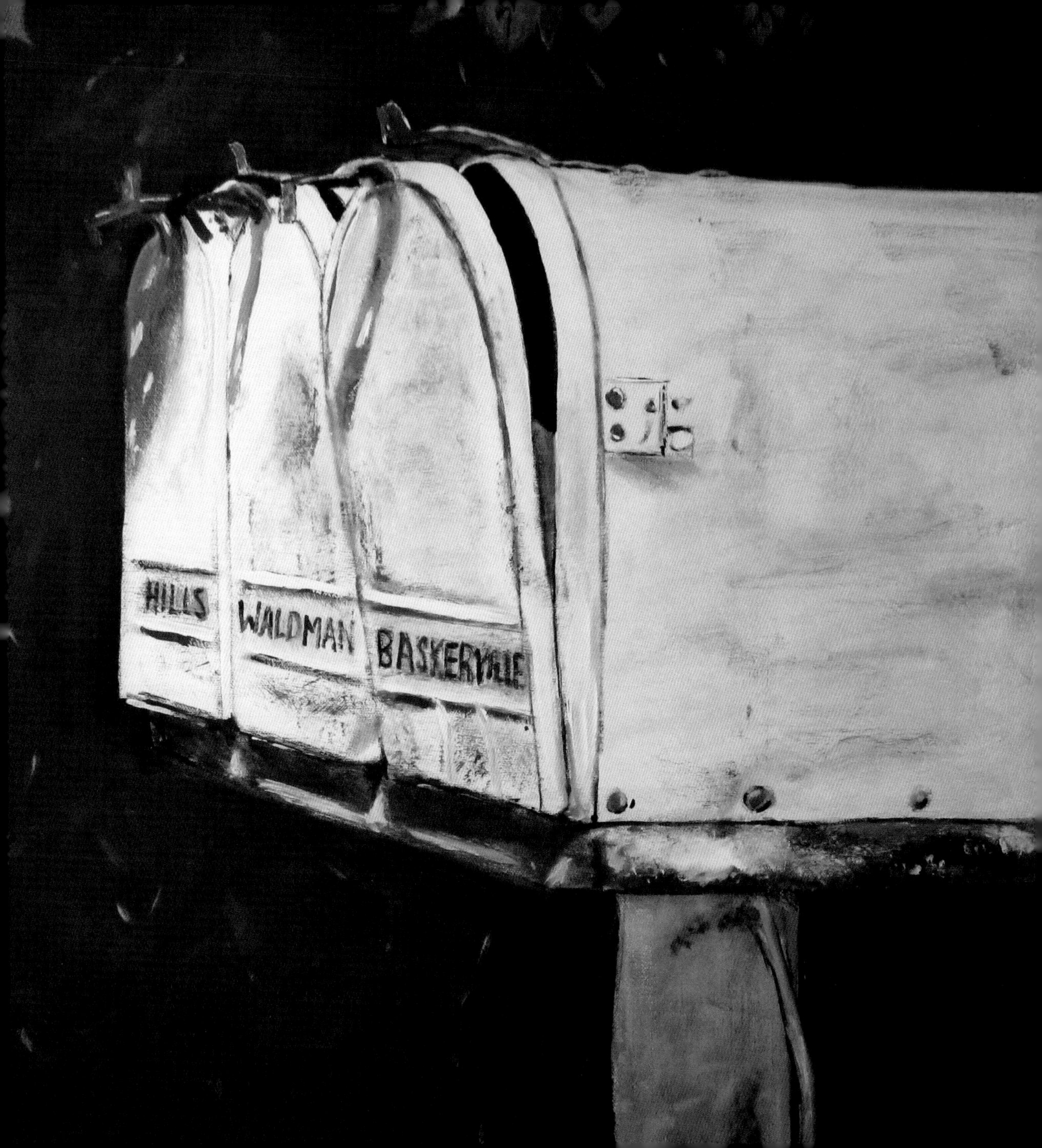
HILLS
WALDMAN
BASKERVILLE

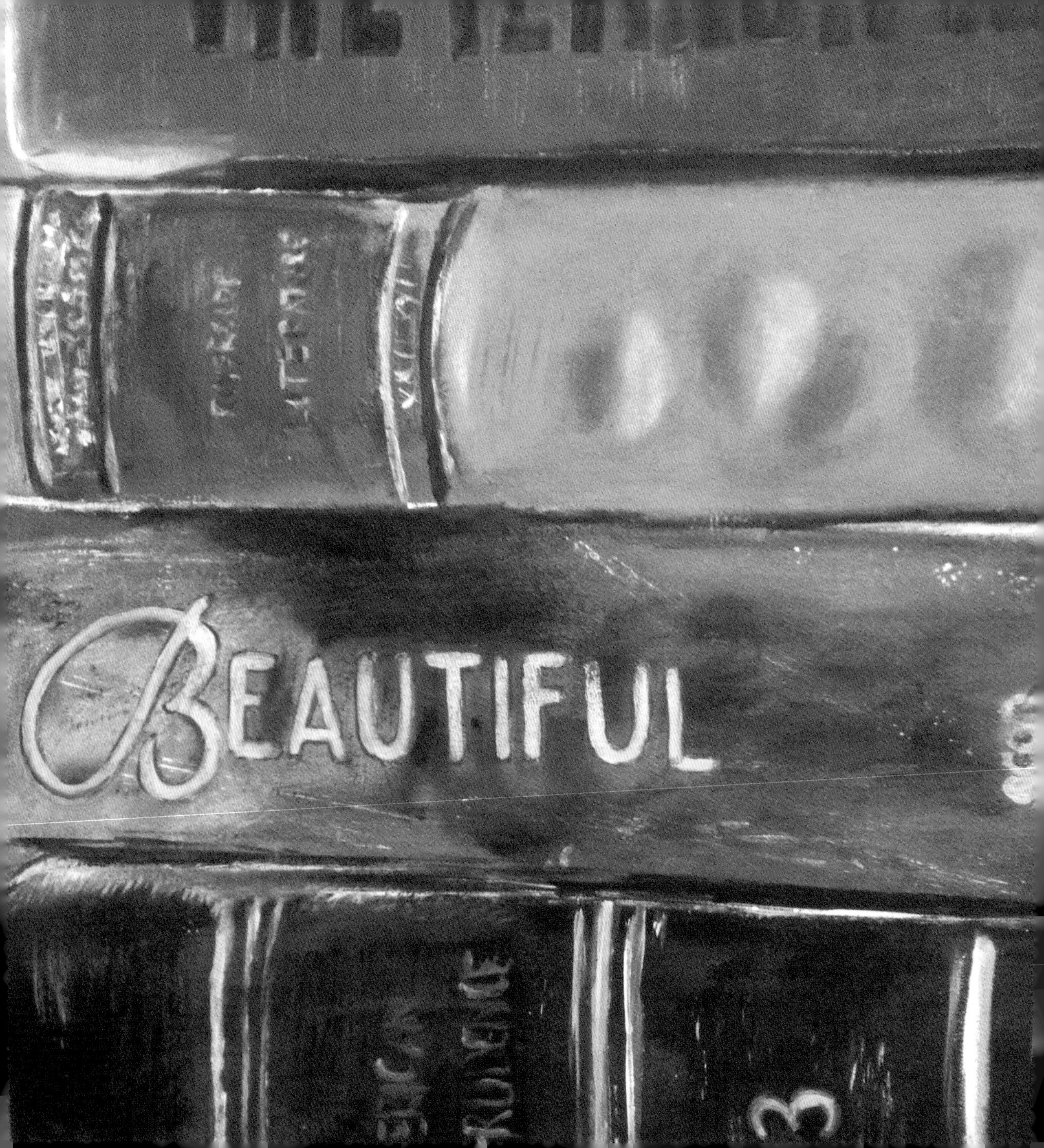
BEAUTIFUL

This place filled with dog-eared books

and lost socks wraps me in a blanket of

"I don't care how you got here."

My heart rests and my wind wanders.

This comfort draws me in...this comfort sets me free. It gives me the confidence to travel a world filled with impermanence and no forwarding address...with paths that change continuously and directions offered only in a whisper. It gives me the wisdom to know rocks in shoes are as much gifts as well lit roadways - all a part of this yearly, this daily, this hourly, this constant journey home.

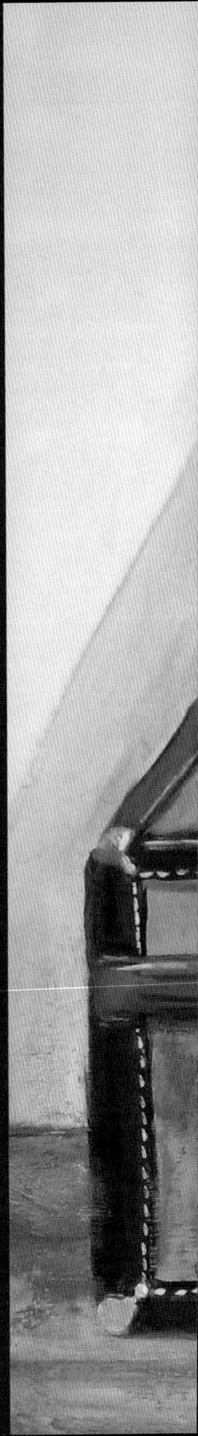

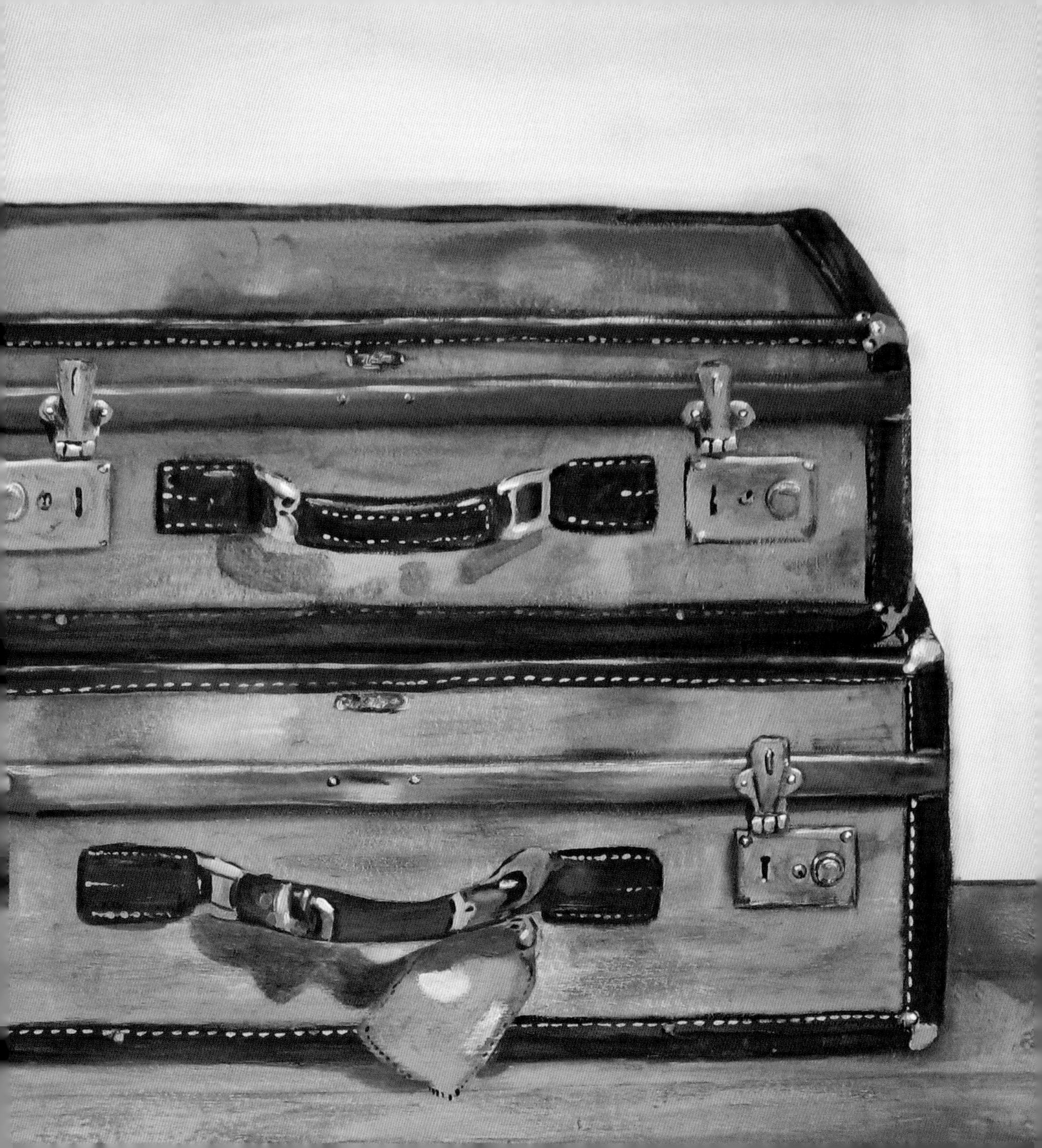

*I*t never complains when I return mud-tracked and weathered.

I approach the entry, and know all is as it has to be...I open the

door and a calm filled grace stops a bit of time, and I sigh. No

judgments, I am held in the believing, comforting, unconditional

arms of this place, and I am welcomed home.

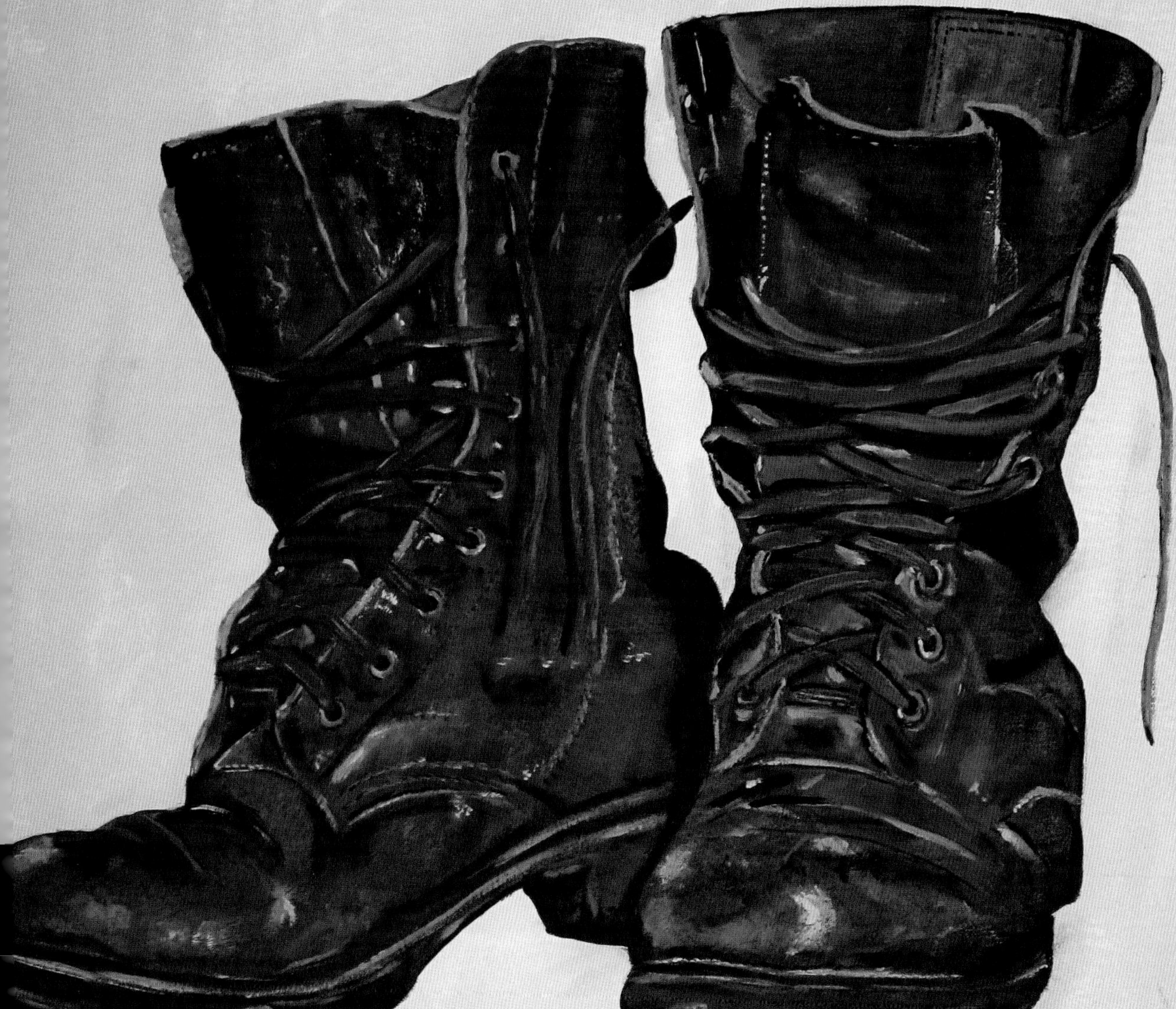

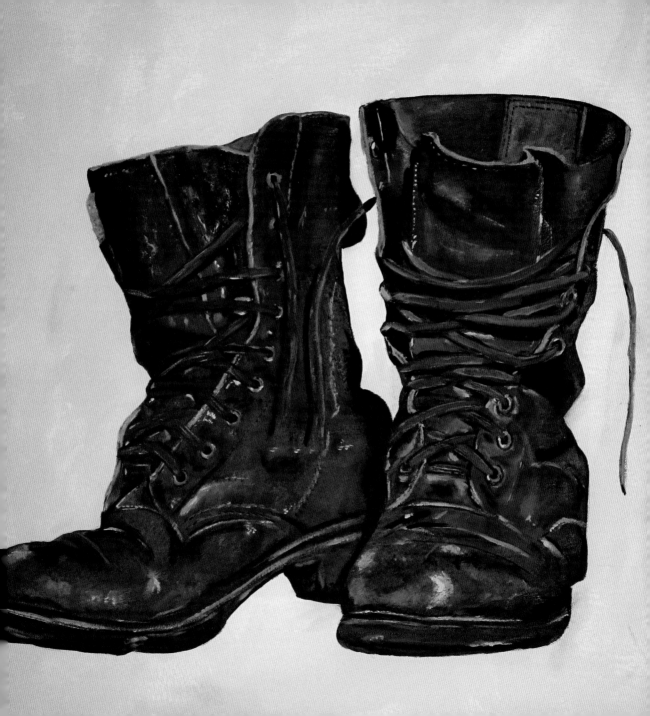

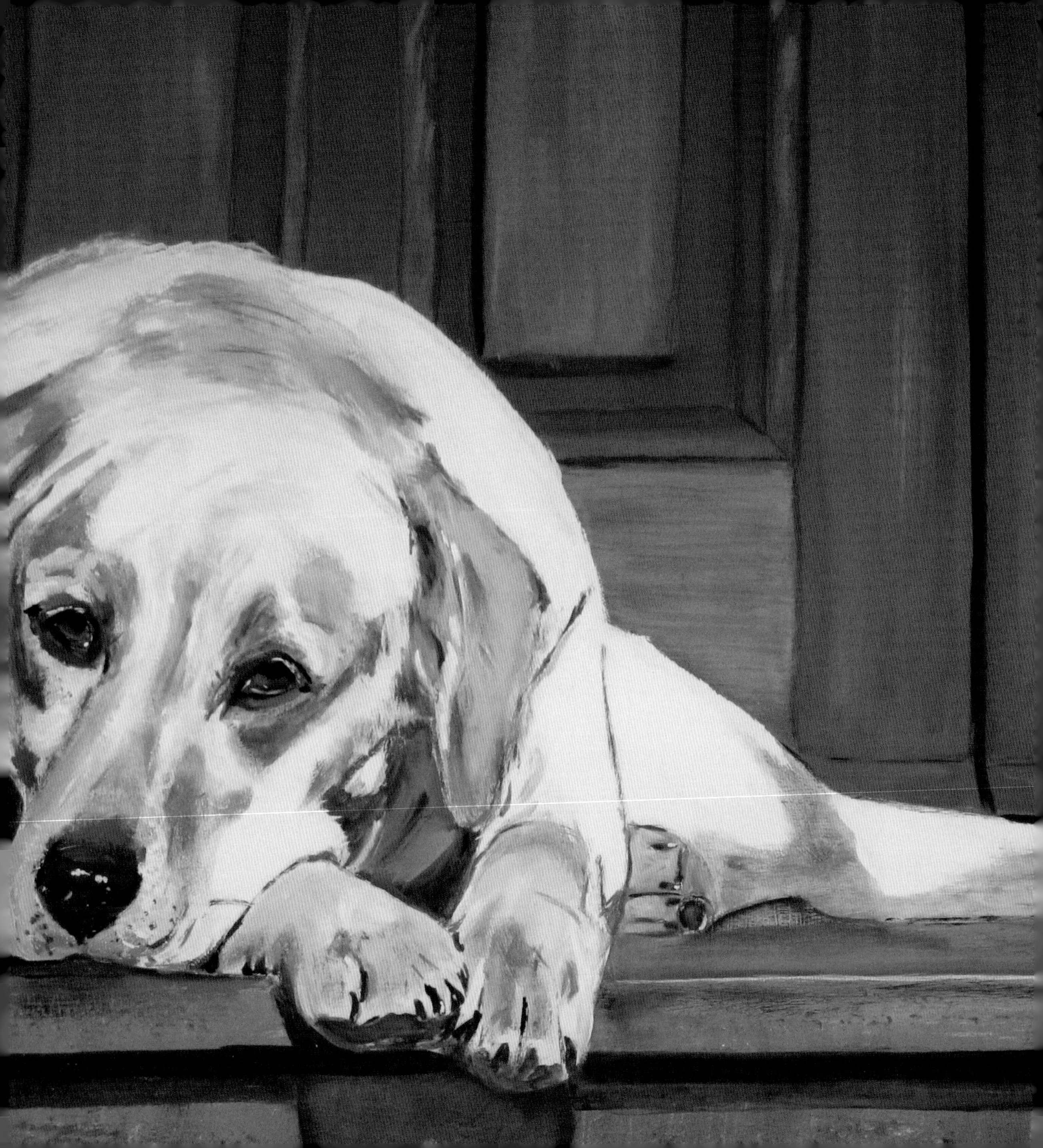

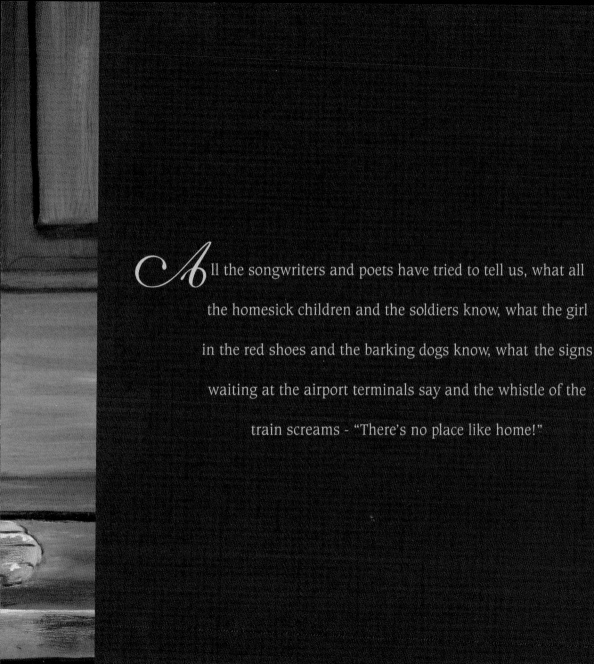

*A*ll the songwriters and poets have tried to tell us, what all

the homesick children and the soldiers know, what the girl

in the red shoes and the barking dogs know, what the signs

waiting at the airport terminals say and the whistle of the

train screams - "There's no place like home!"

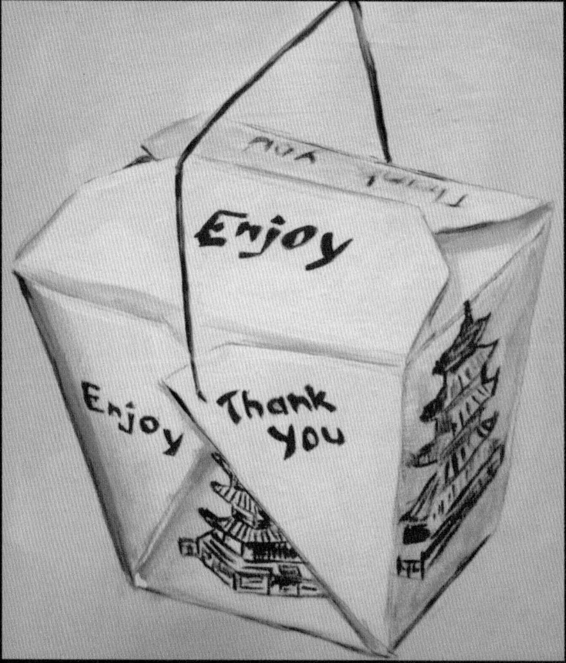

Enjoy
Enjoy
Thank You
Thank You

This place...this home, where else can I truly be known?

This shower has heard me sing. This floor has forgiven my

dance. This refrigerator knows I didn't make all those meals

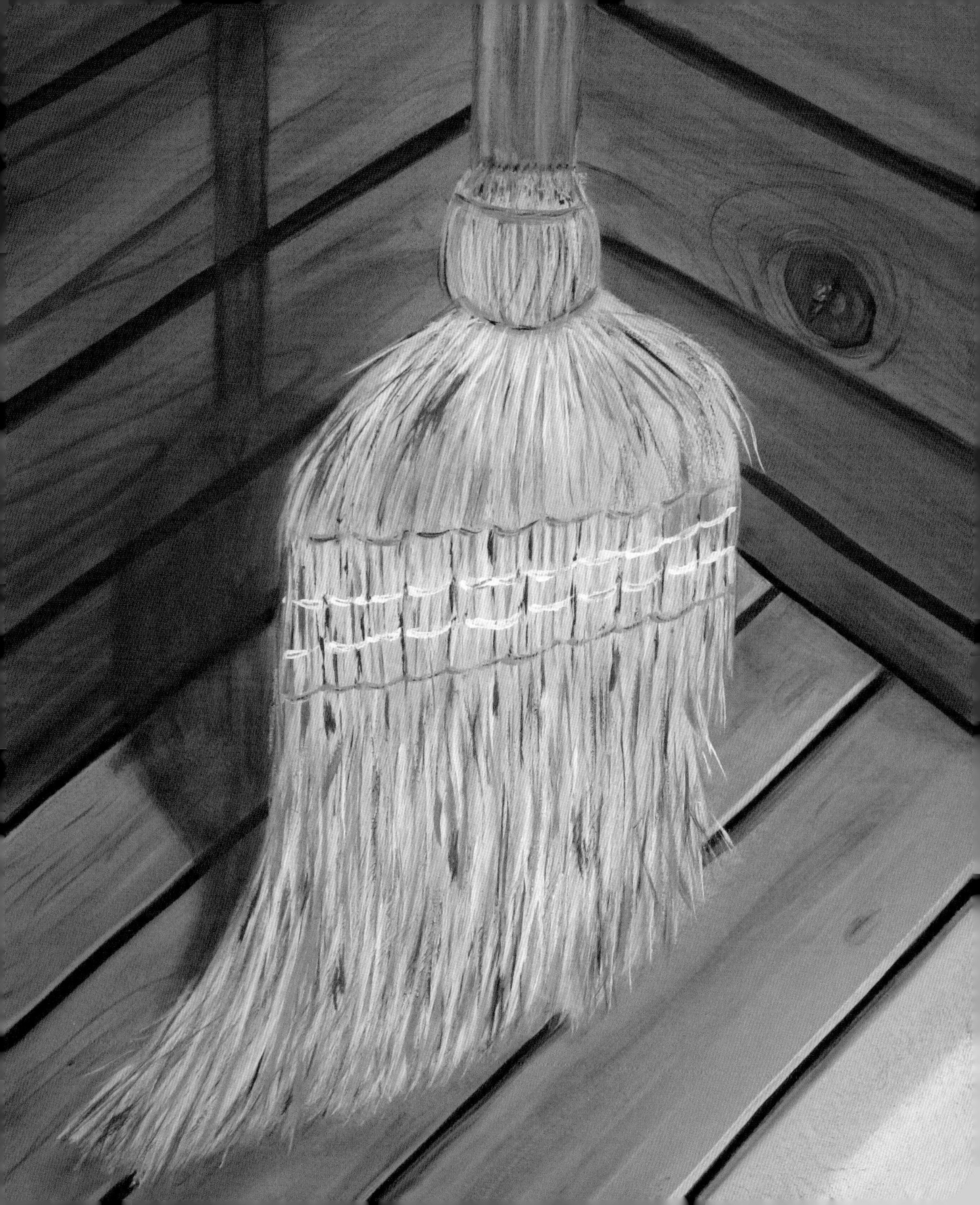

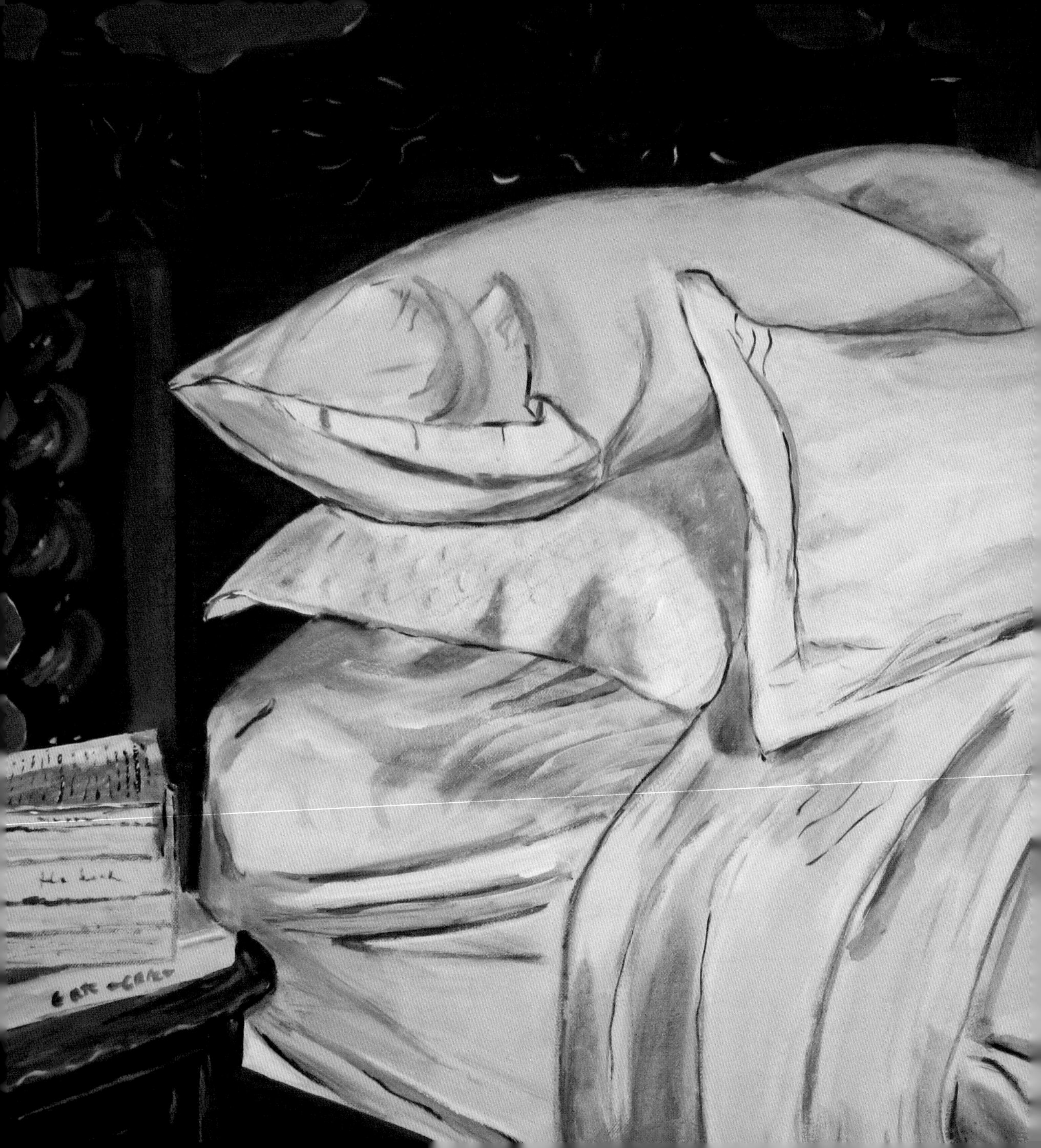

This bed tells me everything will be OK in the morning. These windows have opened my eyes. These mirrors have smiled back.

These stairs know my every step. I climb. I hope. I reach. I pray.

I curse. I kick. I laugh. I rest. I climb. I hope.

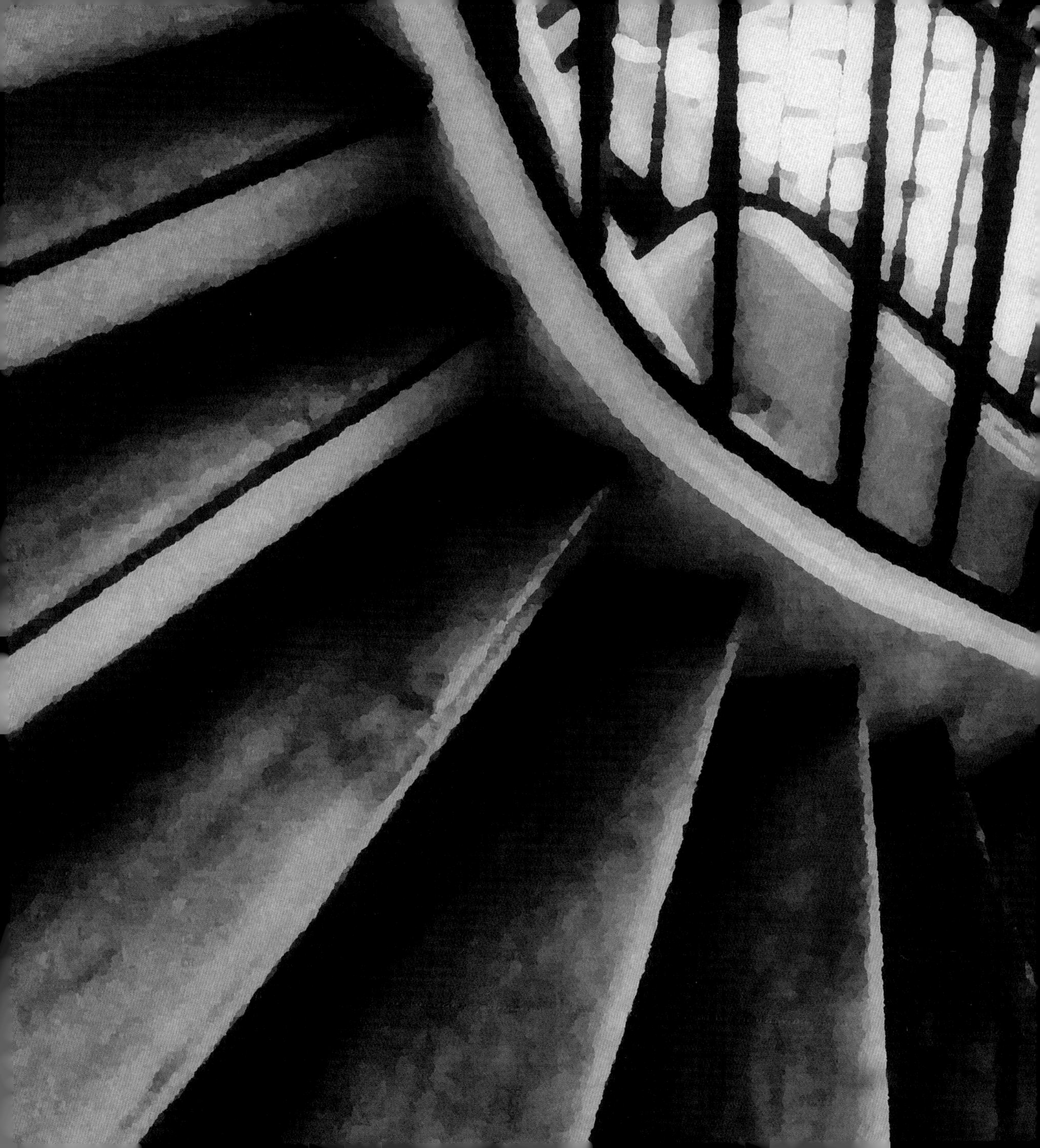

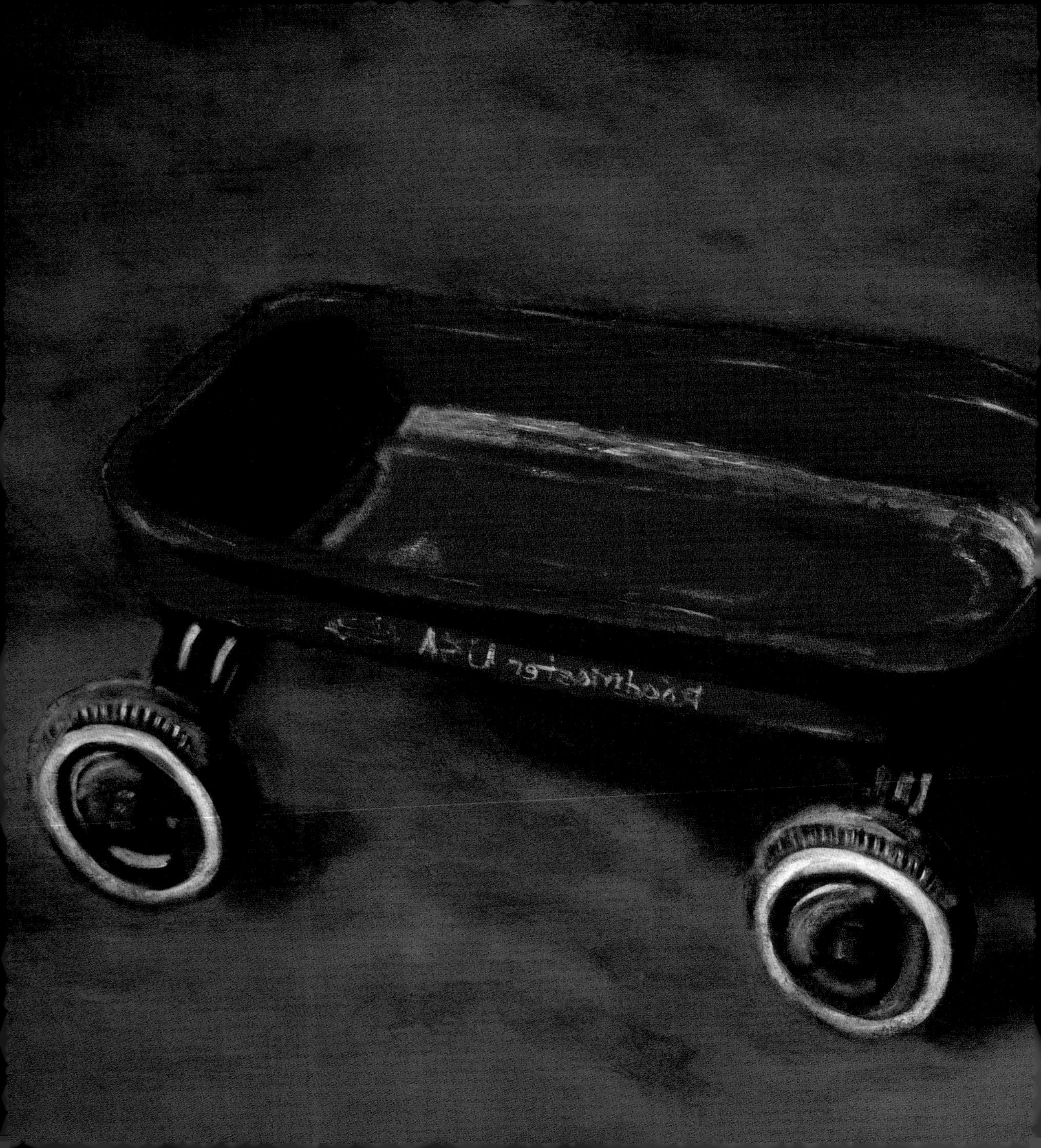

This place knows my life. My home knows the many ways I've tried...what I've let in, and what I've let go...what I've cherished and never forgotten. This place launches my dreams and holds my heart. Here, I am not only allowed to be me, but encouraged. All that I am, and ever was, all that I want to be...this is known at my home.

$\mathcal{O}$h, be it ever so humble, and the universe knows that it

has to be, that I have to be. I have to be able to live in,

live through, and live on...and this will be the story of

home...told in wee hours, rainstorms, and candlelight...

embellished and embraced, and ever home.

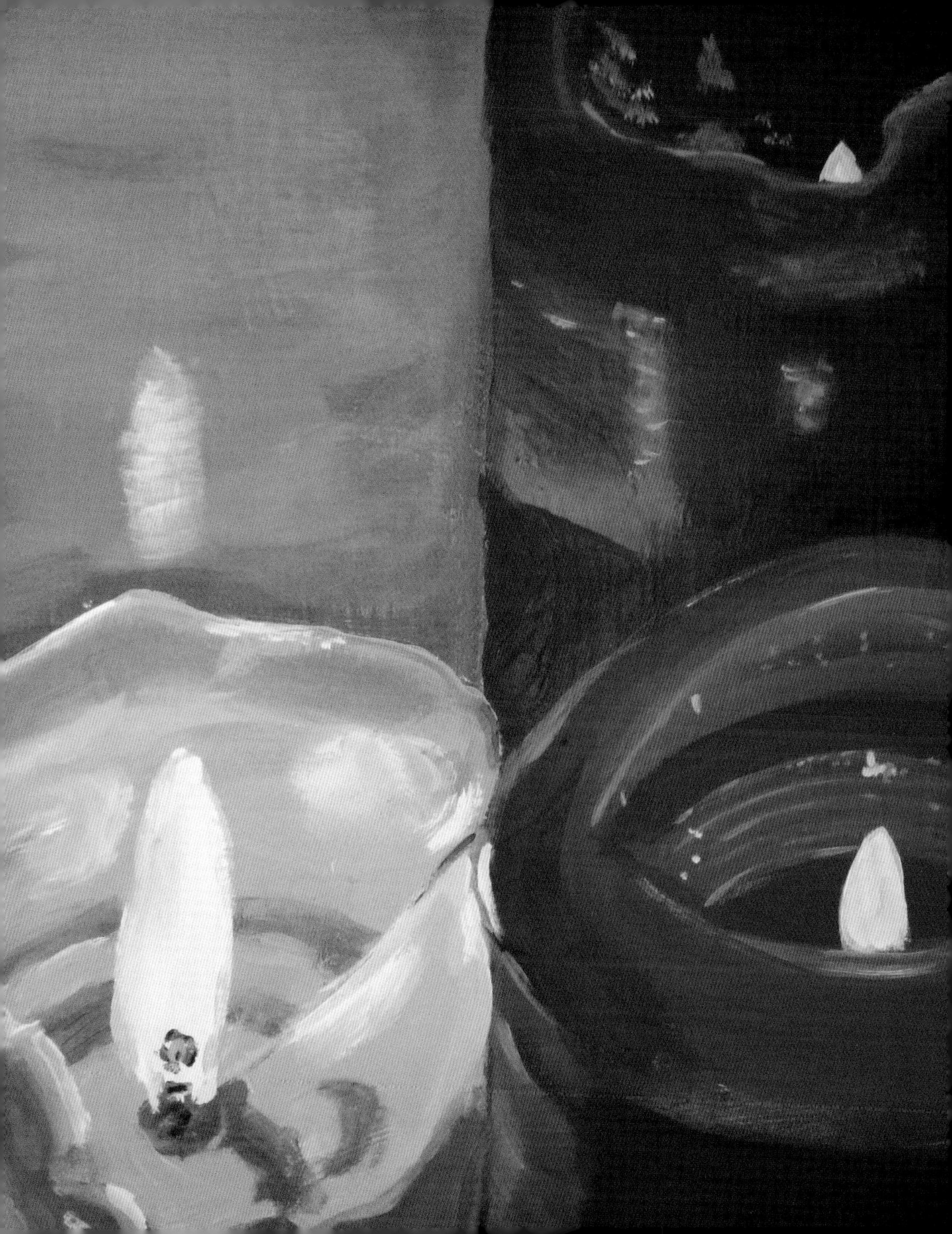

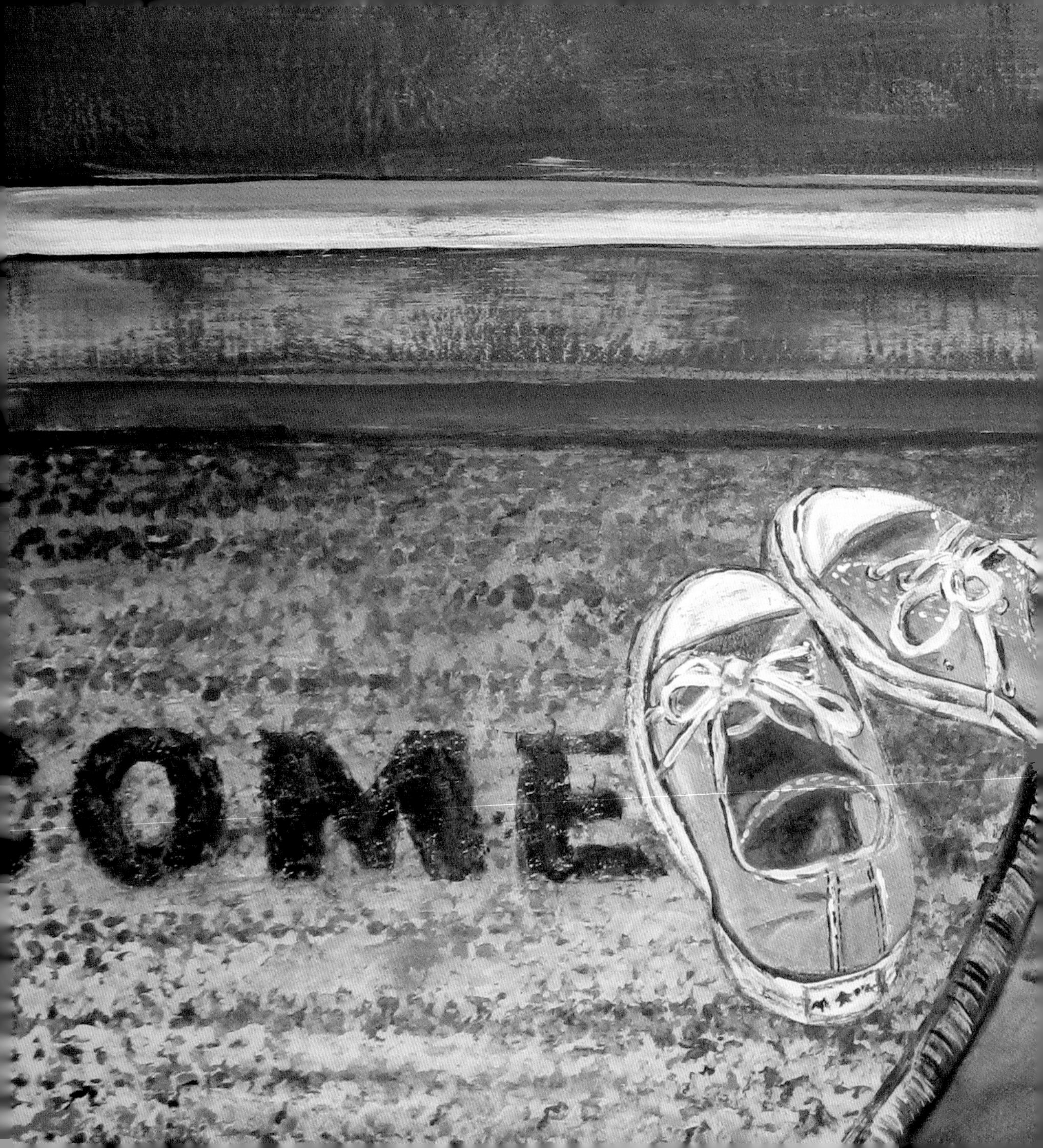
OME

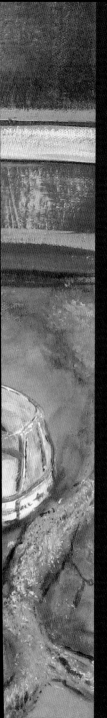

*W*hether my shoes sit singly, or in a cluster of company on the welcome mat, I am not afraid and I am never alone. Through these doors, I become we. Family and friends, loves gained and lost, they are always here in this place...and I am a part of it all.

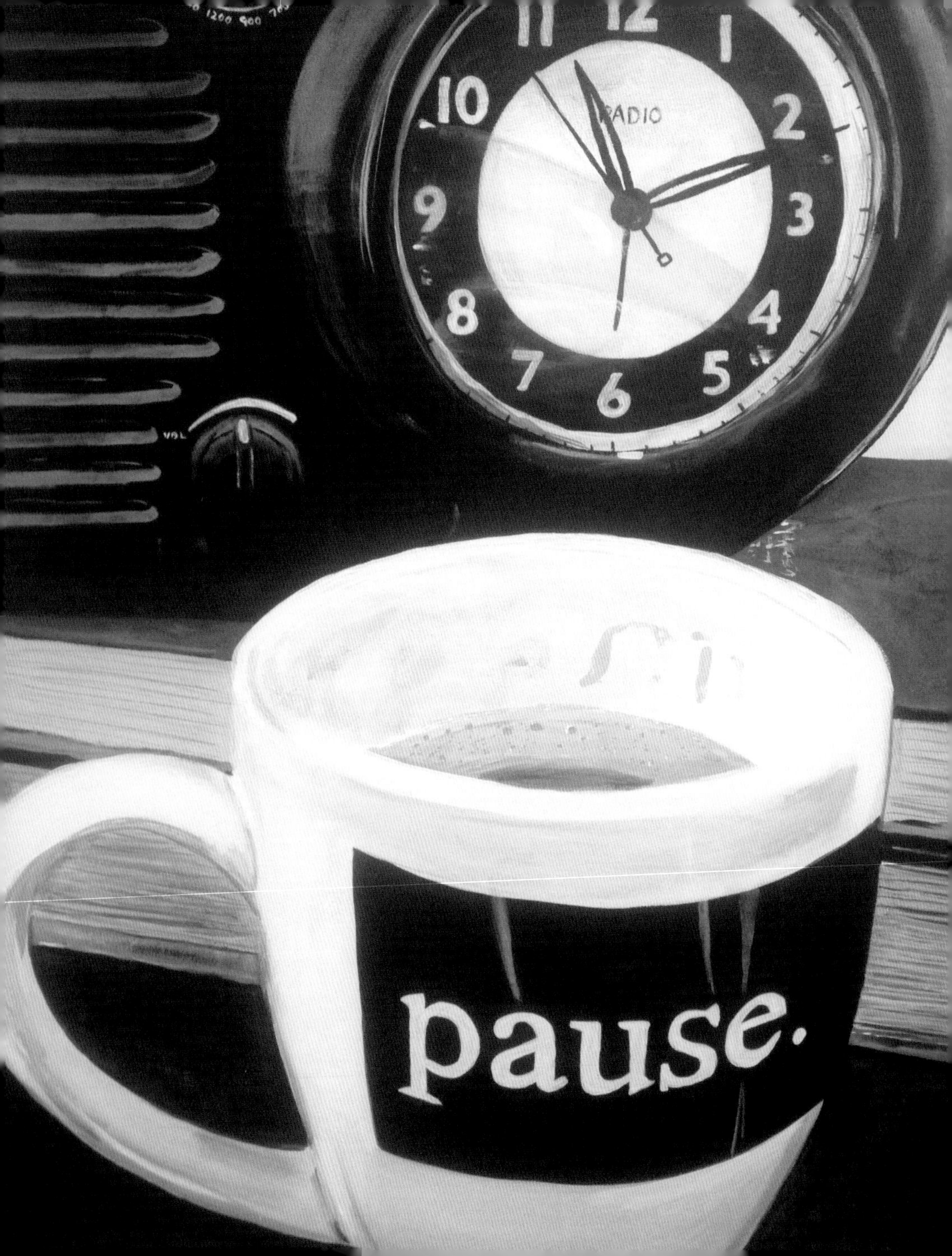
RADIO
VOL
pause.

I am the early morning brew, and the late night snuggle. I am the wishes made over half-burned candles, the ingredients, the left-overs, the crooked pictures, the dreams in the cracked-open windows, the prayers at the edge of bed, the worries under rugs swept.

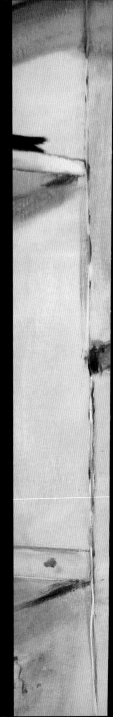

I am part of it all. I am part of the trails that lead to and from here…

the trees, the water, the land…the sidewalks and the buildings. I am

part of the hands waving and horns honking, the birds singing…the

neighbors near and far, all under one sky, trying to get to their own

place of unconditional, outstretched arms.

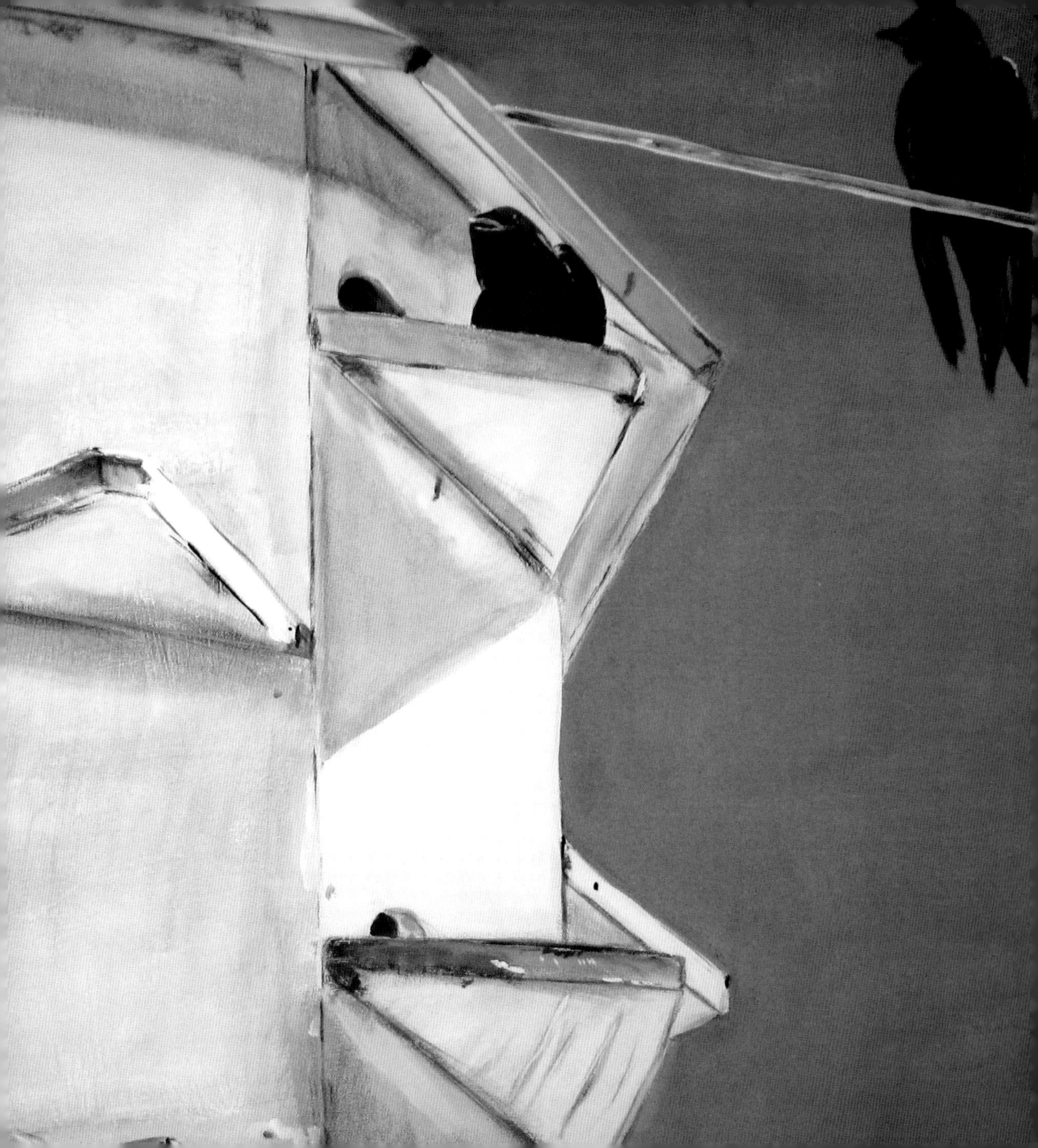

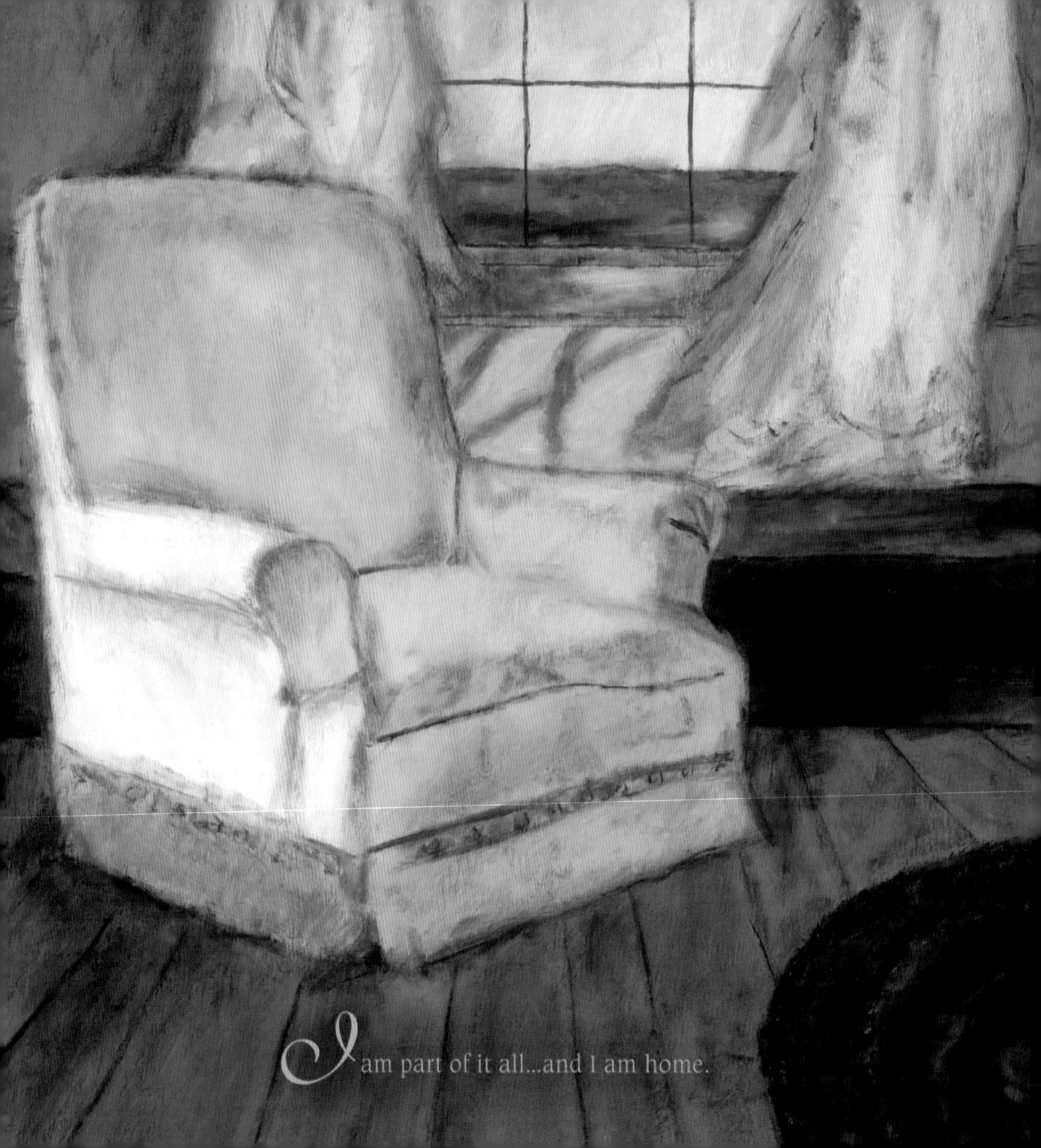

I am part of it all...and I am home.

All the places I've been...I feel like going home.